COLORING TIGER

WORK SUCKS!

An Adult Coloring Book to Relieve Work Stress

MARK THOMPSON

Published in 2017 by Coloring Tiger

Email: mark@coloringtiger.com
Website: www.coloringtiger.com

ISBN-13: 978-0-9996722-0-4
ISBN-10: 0-9996722-0-7

COLORING TIGER ™
Art for Creative Expression

THIS BOOK BELONGS TO

_____

_____

DEAR FRIEND,

Do you ever feel overworked and underappreciated? Do you have stupid co-workers and an unreasonable boss? Does your office feel like a place you can't wait to get out of? Do you need an outlet for bottled up emotions, rage and stress at workplace? Do you ever feel like saying following things:

❖ I wake up with good attitude every day. Then idiots happen.
❖ I am BUSY now. Can I IGNORE you later?
❖ Aw, did I step on your poor itty, bitty ego?
❖ If Monday had a face, I'd punch it.
❖ Well, this day was a total waste of make-up
❖ When did ignorance become a point of view?

If yes, then this coloring book is for you. It has engaging doodle designs containing humorous comments, funny sayings and sarcastic office remarks.

This will help you relieve stress, unwind and relax after a hard day's work. You can even share colored pages with your co-workers, pin them up in your office or, if you're feeling particularly brave, present one to your boss.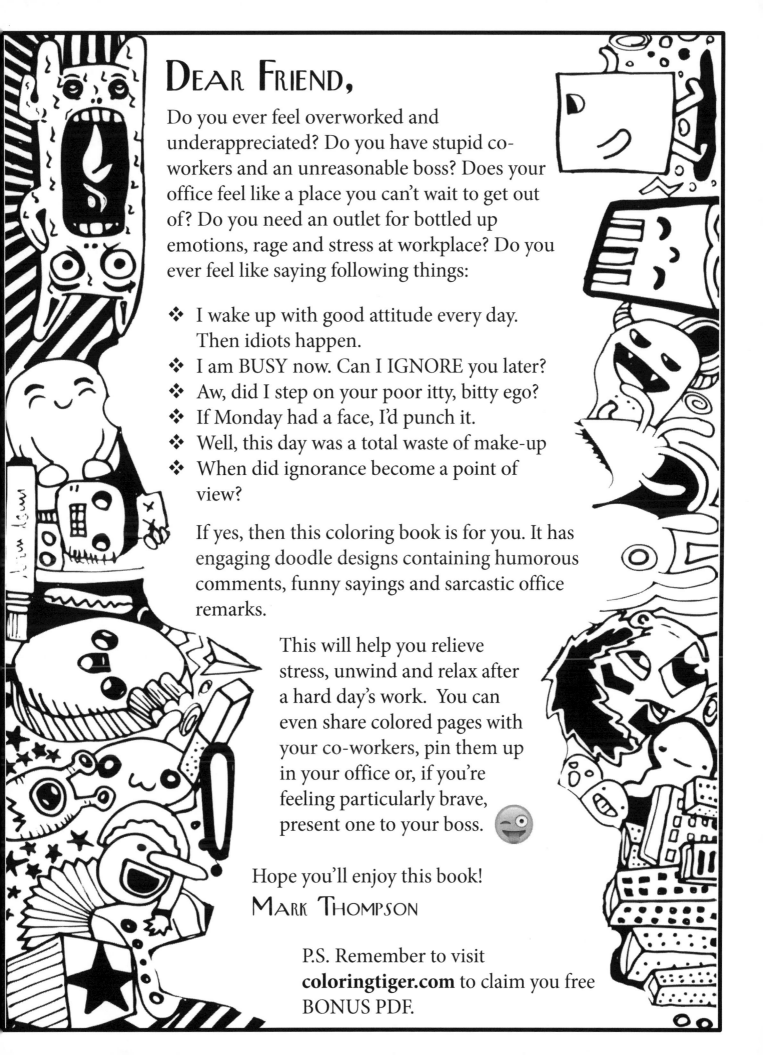

Hope you'll enjoy this book!

MARK THOMPSON

P.S. Remember to visit **coloringtiger.com** to claim you free BONUS PDF.

COLOR TEST PAGE

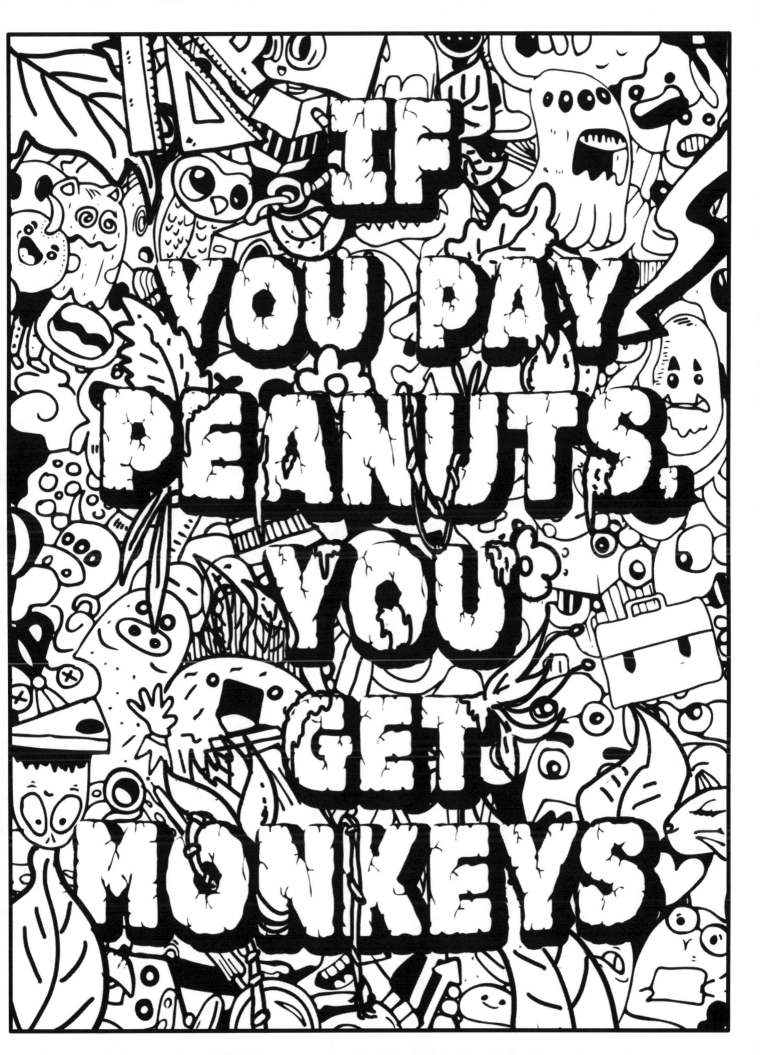

THANK YOU!

WE HOPE YOU LIKED THIS BOOK.

**To stay in touch and download
BONUS PDF please visit**

ColoringTiger.com

Made in the USA
Middletown, DE
28 November 2020